ERING

Stadiums

by Chris Bowman

BELLWETHER MEDIA • MINNEAPOLIS, MN

BLASTOFF!
2
READERS

Note to Librarians, Teachers, and Parents:

Blastoff! Readers are carefully developed by literacy experts and combine standards-based content with developmentally appropriate text.

Level 1 provides the most support through repetition of high-frequency words, light text, predictable sentence patterns, and strong visual support.

Level 2 offers early readers a bit more challenge through varied simple sentences, increased text load, and less repetition of high-frequency words.

Level 3 advances early-fluent readers toward fluency through increased text and concept load, less reliance on visuals, longer sentences, and more literary language.

Level 4 builds reading stamina by providing more text per page, increased use of punctuation, greater variation in sentence patterns, and increasingly challenging vocabulary.

Level 5 encourages children to move from "learning to read" to "reading to learn" by providing even more text, varied writing styles, and less familiar topics.

Whichever book is right for your reader, Blastoff! Readers are the perfect books to build confidence and encourage a love of reading that will last a lifetime!

This edition first published in 2019 by Bellwether Media, Inc.

No part of this publication may be reproduced in whole or in part without written permission of the publisher. For information regarding permission, write to Bellwether Media, Inc., Attention: Permissions Department, 6012 Blue Circle Drive, Minnetonka, MN 55343.

Library of Congress Cataloging-in-Publication Data

Names: Bowman, Chris, 1990- author.
Title: Stadiums / by Chris Bowman.
Description: Minneapolis, MN : Bellwether Media, Inc., 2019. | Series:
  Blastoff! Readers. Everyday Engineering | Includes bibliographical
  references and index. | Audience: Ages 5-8. | Audience: Grades K to 8.
Identifiers: LCCN 2018000224 (print) | LCCN 2018002076 (ebook) | ISBN
  9781626178267 (hardcover : alk. paper) | ISBN 9781681035673 (ebook)
Subjects: LCSH: Stadiums–Juvenile literature.
Classification: LCC TH4714 (ebook) | LCC TH4714 .B69 2019 (print) | DDC 725/.827–dc23
LC record available at https://lccn.loc.gov/2018000224

Editor: Paige V. Polinsky   Designer: Jeffrey Kollock

Printed in the United States of America, North Mankato, MN

Table of Contents

What Are Stadiums?

tiers

Stadiums are large buildings often used for sports or concerts.

Their centers are big open fields. **Tiers** of seats wrap around these spaces.

5

Many early stadiums
were built for races or fights.
Others were for music and plays.

They were made of stone or brick. Some also used **concrete**.

Stadiums today are larger and stronger.

steel

They are still built with concrete.
But steel gives them extra strength.

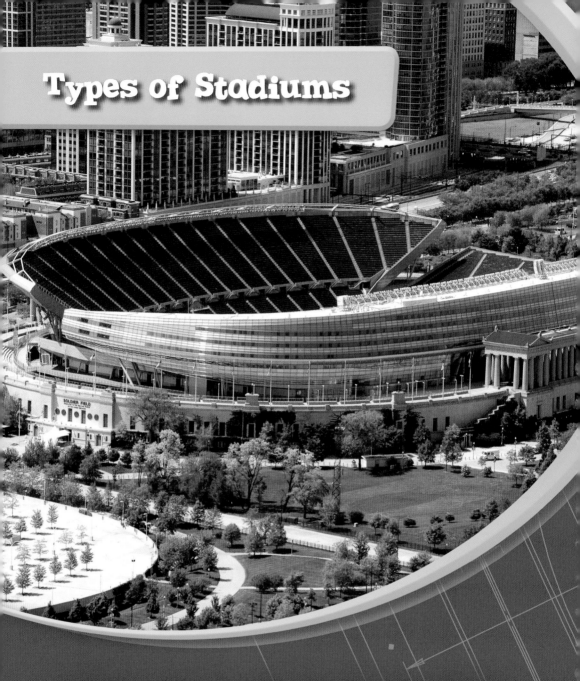

Types of Stadiums

Some stadiums do not have roofs.
The field and seats are all outside.

Others have **retractable** roofs. These can close in bad weather.

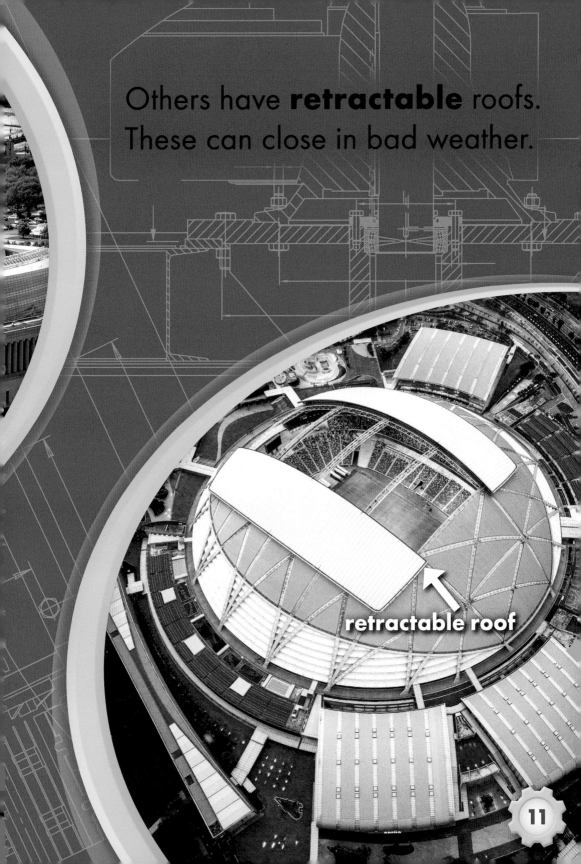

retractable roof

Many stadiums have **fixed** roofs. Some are dome roofs that cover entire buildings.

Others are **cantilever** roofs. These only cover the crowd!

cantilever roof

FAMOUS STRUCTURE PROFILE
U.S. Bank Stadium

Location: Minneapolis, Minnesota
Type: fixed roof stadium
Year Completed: 2016
Architect: John Hutchings; HKS, Inc.
Floor Size: 137,000 square feet
(12,728 square meters)
Seats: up to 70,000

Sometimes stadiums use cable-stay roofs. Cables hang from tall posts to **support** these roofs.

cable-stay roof

trusses

Other stadiums have steel **trusses**. These beams make their roofs extra strong.

Air Pressure at Work

cloth

air pressure

weight

Some stadiums have roofs made of special cloth.

Weights hold the roof to the building. **Air pressure** lifts it and holds it up!

How Do Stadiums Work?

live load

Stadiums sit on top of concrete or rock. These strong bases hold their **dead load**.

Steel beams and **columns** support stadium seats. These help hold moving **live loads**.

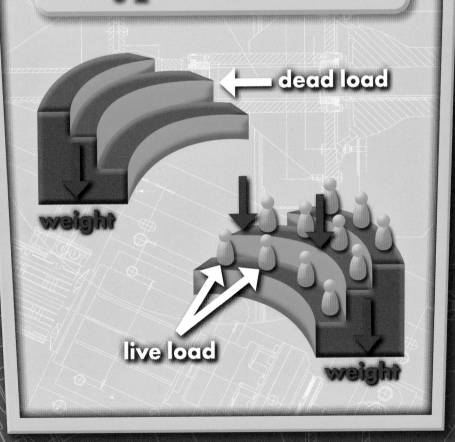

Types of Loads

dead load

weight

live load

weight

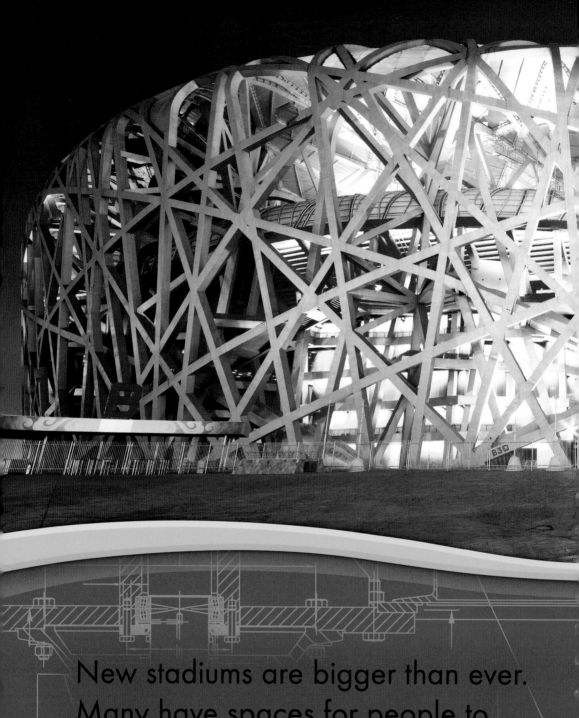

New stadiums are bigger than ever.
Many have spaces for people to
eat and shop.

These giant buildings
keep fans cheering!

Glossary

air pressure—the force of air pushing against something

cantilever—a long object that sticks out from a wall or other object to stretch out over an area

columns—upright beams

concrete—a hard building material made of stone, cement, and water

dead load—the weight or pressure of a stadium without people

fixed—stays in the same place

live loads—the weights or pressures of people inside stadiums

retractable—able to be pulled back

support—to help hold something up

tiers—rows or levels that are placed one above another

trusses—beams shaped like triangles

To Learn More

AT THE LIBRARY

Kelley, K.C. *Stadium*. Mankato, Minn.: Amicus, 2018.

Loh-Hagan, Virginia. *Stadiums*. Ann Arbor, Mich.: Cherry Lake Publishing, 2017.

Pettiford, Rebecca. *Stadiums*. Minneapolis, Minn.: Jump!, Inc., 2016.

ON THE WEB

Learning more about stadiums is as easy as 1, 2, 3.

1. Go to www.factsurfer.com.

2. Enter "stadiums" into the search box.

3. Click the "Surf" button and you will see a list of related web sites.

With factsurfer.com, finding more information is just a click away.

Index

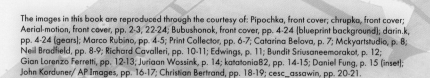